# Lost!

By Joy Cowley

Illustrated by Bert Jackson

⟳ Dominie Press, Inc.

Publisher: Christine Yuen
Editor: John S. F. Graham
Designer: Lois Stanfield
Illustrator: Bert Jackson

Published by:

🔁 **Dominie Press, Inc.**

1949 Kellogg Avenue
Carlsbad, California 92008 USA

www.dominie.com

Paperback ISBN 0-7685-1078-3
Library Bound Edition ISBN 0-7685-1497-5
Printed in Singapore by PH Productions Pte Ltd
  2 3 4 5 6 PH 04 03

# Table of Contents

## Chapter One

# Stay Together

The store was so big,
a jumbo jet could get lost in it.
"Stay by the toys," Mom said to me
and my little sister.
"Look, but don't touch."

"Sure," I said.

Mom looked at me.

"Take good care of her, Buster,"
she said.

Then she crouched down
by my little sister.

"Sarah, stay by Buster.

Don't wander away, okay?"

My little sister nodded.

"I'm going to buy a sunhat," said Mom.
"I'll be back in ten minutes.
Tell me! What do you have to do?"

"Stay together!" we answered.

It was easier to say it than to do it.
The toy department was huge.

I wanted to look at video games.
Sarah wanted to look at
stick-on fingernails.

Video games and fingernails
were not near each other.

"What's that?" Sarah asked.

"Zegog and the Fire Monster," I replied.

"That's silly!" she said.

"No," I said.
"Purple fingernails are silly."

Sarah stomped her feet
and scrunched up her eyes.
"I hate video games," she howled.

"And I hate stick-on claws!" I said.

That did it. She really bellowed.

Chapter Two

# The Juggler

**P**eople were watching us,
and Sarah wouldn't hush up.
That meant I'd have to take her
to look at fingernails and hair ties
and other little kid stuff.

But then I saw a juggler
on the sidewalk, outside the store.
She was dressed like a clown.
She was throwing clubs and balls
into the air and catching them.
I pointed. "Look at that!"

My little sister closed her mouth
and un-scrunched her eyes.

With a happy shout,
she ran out the store door.
She went right up to the juggler,
who looked down at her and smiled.

There were heaps of people
on the sidewalk.
I grabbed my little sister's hand.
"You can watch if you don't howl,"
I said.

I didn't know how that juggler
kept all that stuff up in the air.
First, there were the bats and balls.
Then there were cups and saucers.
They were made of real china, too.
If they dropped, they'd be smashed.

I didn't notice that
Sarah had let go of my hand.
I said, "Maybe I'll buy juggling balls,"
and I turned toward her.
But Sarah wasn't there.
My little sister had gone!

## Chapter Three

# A Blue Jacket and Messy Hair

**S**arah wasn't anywhere
on the sidewalk.
I ran into the store
and went up and down
the toy department, looking for her.

She wasn't by the stick-on fingernails.
She wasn't anywhere.
"Excuse me," I said to the man
behind the toy counter.
"Have you seen a little girl
with a blue jacket and messy hair?
She's three, and she's got freckles."

No, the man hadn't seen Sarah.

I went back to the street.

I was really worried.

"Sarah!" I called. "Sarah! Sarah!"

The juggler stopped juggling.

"My little sister!" I said. "I've lost her!"

The juggler was very kind.
So were the people on the sidewalk.
But all the kindness in the world
didn't tell me where Sarah was.

Had she gone into another store?
Had she tried to cross the street?

Then Mom came out of the store,
looking for me.

I felt awful. "Sarah's gone," I said.
"I don't know where she is."

## Chapter Four

# One Minute She Was Here

**M**om didn't get mad.

She didn't even blame me.

Her face was pale, and she said,

"What happened?"

"She just disappeared," I said.

"She ran away,"
said an elderly woman.

"Ran away?" Mom cried.
"My little Sarah?"

The juggler said,
"Don't worry. She can't be far away."

"We've looked around the block,"
a man said to Mom.

Now Mom was shaking.

"We have to call the police!"

"I was holding her hand, Mom,"
I said. "One minute she was here.
The next minute..."

"It's all right, Buster," said Mom.
"It's not your fault.
She can run like greased lightning."

Mom went back
to the toy department.
She said to the man at the counter,
"My little girl is missing.
I want to call the police.
Please, may I use your phone?"

"Of course," the man said.

## Chapter Five

# Come with Me

**B**efore Mom could pick up the phone,
a store security guard came up.
"Excuse me," she said to Mom.
"Are you the woman who's looking
for a little girl in a blue jacket?"

"My daughter Sarah!" Mom cried.

"About three years old?"
said the security guard.

Mom grabbed the woman's sleeve.
"Have you seen her?"

The security guard smiled.
"Would you like to come with me?"

She led us away from the toys,
through children's clothing,
past shoes, past lamps,
past kitchen stuff,
past tables and chairs,
to the place where the beds were.

My little sister was lying on a bed,
fast asleep, her thumb in her mouth.

I didn't know whether to laugh
or get mad at her.

"She must have been looking for me,"
said Mom.
"She must have gotten tired."

"I should have
paid more attention to her," I said.

Mom nodded. She was smiling again.
Gently, she shook Sarah.
"Wake up, funny bunny," she said.
"It's time to go home."

My little sister sat up in the store bed,
her hair messier than ever.

She looked at Mom, then me,
and her eyes scrunched up.
Her mouth slowly opened.
"Fingernails!" she yelled.

Mom said, "What does she mean?"

I pulled Sarah off the bed.
"Okay!" I said to her. "Let's look
at the stick-on fingernails."

Sarah looked up at me.
She was all smiles.
"I love you, Buster," she said.